Newport Public Library

Nature's Cycles
Food Chains

Los ciclos de la naturaleza
Las cadenas alimentarias

Dana Meachen Rau

 Marshall Cavendish
Benchmark
New York

2

Running! Jumping! Playing!

Where do you get all your *energy*? You get energy for your body from food.

———◆———

¡Corres! ¡Saltas! ¡Juegas!

¿De dónde obtienes toda tu *energía*? Obtienes energía para tu cuerpo de los alimentos.

All living things need food. Food is a type of energy. A *food chain* is the flow of energy from one living thing to the next.

Todos los seres vivos necesitan alimento. El alimento es un tipo de energía. Una *cadena alimentaria* es el flujo de energía de un ser vivo al siguiente.

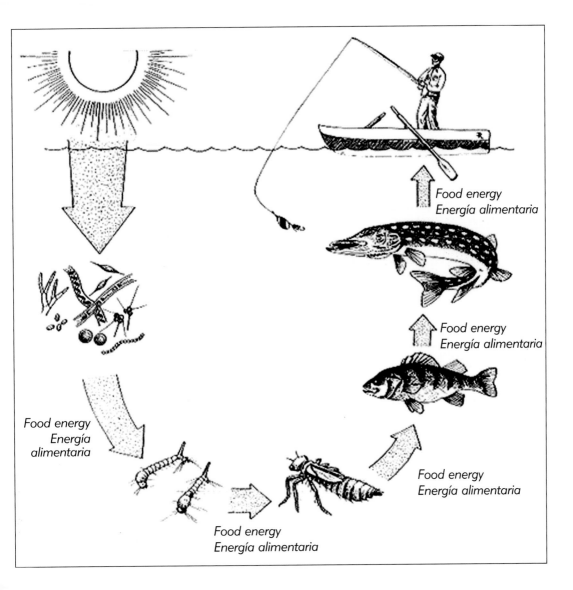

Food energy
Energía alimentaria

Food energy
Energía alimentaria

Food energy
Energía alimentaria

Food energy
Energía alimentaria

5

Plants make their own food. Their leaves take in energy from the sun.

Las plantas producen su propio alimento. Las hojas absorben energía del sol.

Their roots suck water and *nutrients* from the *soil*. They take a gas out of the air. Plants use all these things to make food.

Las raíces absorben agua y *nutrientes* del *suelo*. Toman un gas del aire. Las plantas usan todas estas cosas para producir alimento.

Animals cannot make their own food. They need to find food to eat so they can live.

Los animales no pueden producir su propio alimento. Necesitan encontrar alimento que comer para poder vivir.

Some animals eat plants to get energy. Cows and horses eat grass.

———❖———

Algunos animales comen plantas para obtener energía. Las vacas y los caballos comen hierba.

Pandas feed on stalks of bamboo.

Los pandas se alimentan de tallos de bambú.

Some animals eat meat to get energy. Spiders catch flies in webs.

❖

Algunos animales comen carne para obtener energía. Las arañas atrapan moscas en sus telarañas.

Snakes hunt for mice. Vultures eat animals that
have died.

Las serpientes cazan ratones. Los buitres comen
animales que han muerto.

Some animals eat both plants and animals.
Berries and fish are food for a bear. Nuts and
crabs can feed a raccoon. Kids eat plants and
animals, too. The food you eat gives you energy.

——————❖——————

Algunos animales comen plantas y animales.
Para un oso, son alimento las bayas y los peces.
Un mapache puede alimentarse de nueces
y cangrejos. Los niños también comen plantas y
animales. Los alimentos que comes te dan energía.

All living things die. Plants turn brown and fall to the ground.

Todos los seres vivos mueren. Las plantas se secan y caen al suelo.

Animals do not live forever either. Some animals are eaten by other animals. Other animals die when they get old.

Los animales tampoco viven para siempre.
Algunos animales comen a otros animales.
Otros animales mueren cuando llegan a viejos.

Dead plants and animals *decay*. Mushrooms grow on a dead log. They help turn the log into soil. The soil is rich with nutrients. New plants use the nutrients to grow.

———❖———

Las plantas y los animales muertos se *descomponen*. Los hongos crecen sobre un tronco muerto. Ayudan a convertir el tronco en suelo. El suelo es rico en nutrientes. Las plantas nuevas usan los nutrientes para crecer.

Animals that hunt and eat other animals are *predators*. The animals they eat are *prey*.

———◆———

Los animales que cazan y comen a otros animales son *predadores*. Los animales que ellos comen son las *presas*.

No one eats the top predator in a food chain. The predator will die and decay. Its energy is given back to the soil.

❖

Nadie come al predador que está en la cima de una cadena alimentaria. El predador se morirá y se descompondrá. Su energía regresa al suelo.

Look at a food chain in a pond. A fish eats plants.

❖

Mira la cadena alimentaria de una laguna.
Un pez come plantas.

An alligator eats the fish. When the alligator dies, it falls to the bottom. When it decays, it helps new plants grow.

Un aligator se come al pez. Cuando el aligator muere, cae al fondo. Cuando se descompone, ayuda a crecer a las plantas nuevas.

Look at a food chain in a field. A cricket
eats grass.

Mira la cadena alimentaria de un prado.
Un grillo come hierba.

A bird eats the cricket. The bird dies and decays.
This feeds the soil so the grass can grow.

Un pájaro se come al grillo. El pájaro muere y
se descompone. Esto alimenta al suelo para que
pueda crecer hierba.

In food chains, different animals eat the same foods. A predator may eat more than one kind of plant or animal. The food chains mix together. This is a *food web*.

En las cadenas alimentarias, animales diferentes comen los mismos alimentos. Un predador puede comer más de una clase de planta o animal. Las cadenas alimentarias se mezclan. Esto es una *red alimentaria*.

Living things need each other. When they die,
they help other living things grow.

Los seres vivos se necesitan unos a otros. Cuando
mueren, ayudan a crecer a otros seres vivos.

Challenge Words

decay—To break down into nutrients for the soil.

energy—The power to do work.

food chain—The flow of energy from one living thing to the next.

food web—The criss-cross flow of energy among animals and plants in an area.

nutrients—A food material needed for growth.

predator—An animal that hunts and eats other animals.

prey—An animal that is eaten by another animal.

soil—The earth in which plants grow.

Palabras avanzadas

cadena alimentaria—El flujo de energía de un ser vivo al siguiente.

descomponer—Desintegrarse en nutrientes para el suelo.

energía—La fuerza para trabajar.

nutrientes—Material alimenticio necesario para crecer.

predador—Animal que caza y come a otros animales.

presa—Animal al que come otro animal.

red alimentaria—El flujo de energía entrecruzado entre animales y plantas de un área.

suelo—La tierra en la que crecen las plantas.

Index

Page numbers in **boldface** are illustrations.

air, 7
alligator, 23, **23**
animals, **8**, 9, 10, **10**, **11**, 12, 13, 15, 20, **20**, **21**, 26, **27**
  dead, 13, 17, 18, **21**, 23, 25, 29

bamboo, 11, **11**
bears, 15
birds, 25, **25**, 27, **28**

cows, 10
cricket, 24, **24**, 25, **25**

decay, 18, 21, 23, 25, 30
deer, **27**

eating, **8**, 9–10, **10**, **11**, 12, **12**, 13, **14**, 15, 17, 20–26, **22**, **23**, **25**
energy, 3, 4, **5**, 6, 10, 12, 15, 21, 30

fish, 22, **22**, 23, **23**
flies, 12, **12**
food, 3–7, **5**, 9, **14**, 15, 26
food chain, 4, **5**, 21, 26, 30
  field, 24–25, **24**, **25**
  pond, 22–23, **22**, **23**
food web, 26, 30

gas, 7
giraffe, **8**
grass, 10, **10**, 24, **24**, 25

growing, 18, 23, 25, 29

horses, 10, **10**
hunting, 13, 20, **20**

kids, **14**, 15

leaves, 6, **6**, **8**

meat eaters, 12
mice, 13, **13**
mushrooms, 18, **19**

nutrients, 7, 18, 30

pandas, 11, **11**
plants, 6–7, **6**, **7**, 10, **10**, **11**, 15, 22, **22**, 23, 26
  dead, 16, **16**, 18, 29
predator, 20–21, **20**, **21**, 26, 30
prey, 20, **20**, 30

raccoon, 15
roots, 7, **7**

snakes, 13, **13**
soil, 7, **7**, 18, 21, 25, 30
spiders, 12, **12**
sun, 6, **6**

vultures, 13

water, 7
webs, 12, **12**

Índice

Las páginas indicadas con números en **negrita** tienen ilustraciones.

agua, 7
aire, 7
aligator, 23, **23**
alimento, 3–7, **5**, 9, **14**, 15, 26
animales, **8**, 9, 10, **10**, **11**, 12, 13, 15, 20, **20**, **21**, 26, **27**
  muerte, 13, 17, 18, **21**, 23, 25, 29
arañas, 12, **12**

bambú, 11, **11**
buitres, 13

caballos, 10, **10**
cadena alimentaria, 4, **5**, 21, 26, 30
  laguna, 22–23, **22**, **23**
  prado, 24–25, **24**, **25**
cazar, 13, 20, **20**
ciervo, **27**
comedores de carne, 12
comer, **8**, 9–10, **10**, **11**, 12, **12**, 13, **14**, 15, 17, 20–26, **22**, **23**, **25**
crecer, 18, 23, 25, 29

descomponer, 18, 21, 23, 25, 30

energía, 3, 4, **5**, 6, 10, 12, 15, 21, 30

gas, 7
grillo, 24, **24**, 25, **25**

hierba, 10, **10**, 24, **24**, 25
hojas, 6, **6**, **8**
hongos, 18, **19**

jirafa, **8**

mapache, 15
moscas, 12, **12**

niños, **14**, 15
nutrientes, 7, 18, 30

osos, 15

pájaros, 25, **25**, 27, **28**
pandas, 11, **11**
pez, 22, **22**, 23, **23**
plantas, 6–7, **6**, **7**, 10, 10, 11, 15, 22, **22**, 23, 26
  muerte, 16, **16**, 18, 29
predador, 20–21, **20**, **21**, 26, 30
presa, 20, **20**, 30

raíces, 7, **7**
ratones, 13, **13**
red alimentaria, 26, 30

serpientes, 13, **13**
sol, 6, **6**
suelo, 7, **7**, 18, 21, 25, 30

telarañas, 12, **12**

vacas, 10

*The author would like to thank Paula Meachen
for her scientific guidance and expertise in reviewing this book.*

With thanks to Nanci Vargus, Ed.D.,
and Beth Walker Gambro, reading consultants.

Marshall Cavendish Benchmark
99 White Plains Road
Tarrytown, New York 10591
www.marshallcavendish.us

Library of Congress Cataloging-in-Publication Data

Rau, Dana Meachen, 1971–
[Food chains. Spanish & English]
Food chains = Las cadenas alimentarias / Dana Meachen Rau.
p. cm. — (Bookworms. Nature's cycles = Los ciclos de la naturaleza)
Includes index.
Parallel text in English and Spanish; translated from the English.
ISBN 978-0-7614-4789-4 (bilingual ed.) — ISBN 978-0-7614-4095-6 (English ed.)
1. Food chains (Ecology)—Juvenile literature. I. Title. II. Title: Cadenas alimentarias.
QH541.14.R3818 2010
577'.16—dc22
2009019020

Editor: Christina Gardeski
Publisher: Michelle Bisson
Designer: Virginia Pope
Art Director: Anahid Hamparian

Spanish Translation and Text Composition by Victory Productions, Inc.
www.victoryprd.com

Photo Research by Anne Burns Images

Cover Photo by *Photo Researchers*/Linda Freshwaters Amdt

The photographs in this book are used with permission and through the courtesy of:
Animals Animals: pp. 1, 25 ABPL Gerald Hinde. *Getty Images*: p. 2 Sabine Scheckel; p. 6 James French;
p. 8 Anup Shak; p. 10 Richard Ross; p. 11 Keren Su; p. 17 Andrew Holt; p. 19 Tim Graham; p. 20 Getty Images;
p. 21 Time & Life Pictures. *Photri Microstock*: p. 5. *Photo Researchers*: p. 7 Gunilla Elam; p. 16 Nigel Cattlin;
p. 23 James H. Robinson; p. 24 Hans Reinhard; p. 27 Linda Freshwaters Amdt; p. 28 Clem Haagner. *Corbis*:
p. 12 Herbert Kehrer/zefa; p. 13 David A. Northcott. *Photo Edit*: p. 14 Richard Hutchings. *Peter Arnold*: p. 22 BIOS.

Printed in Malaysia
1 3 5 6 4 2